Barn Owls

Nocturnal Hunters

Rebecca Rissman

Raintree is an imprint of Capstone Global Library Limited, a company incorporated in England and Wales having its registered office at 7 Pilgrim Street, London, EC4V 6LB – Registered company number: 6695582

www.raintreepublishers.co.uk
myorders@raintreepublishers.co.uk

Edited by Brynn Baker, Clare Lewis, and
     Helen Cox Cannons
Designed by Kyle Grenz and Tim Bond
Picture research by Tracy Cummins
Production by Helen McCreath
Originated by Capstone Global Library Limited
Printed and bound in China by Leo Paper Group

ISBN 978-1-406-28281-8
18 17 16 15 14
10 9 8 7 6 5 4 3 2 1

British Library Cataloguing in Publication Data
A full catalogue record for this book is available from the British Library.

Acknowledgements
We would like to thank the following for permission to reproduce photographs: FLPA: Derek Middleton, 7 mouse, Erica Olsen, 19, Gary K Smith, 21, Imagebroker, 5, 23d, Michael Durham/Minden Pictures, 7 bat, Paul Sawer, 17, Simon Litten, 20, 23c; Getty Images: Derrick Hamrick, 1, 23g, Oxford Scientific/Michael Leach, front cover; Science Source: Kenneth M. Highfill, 9; Shutterstock: Andrew Astbury, 7 fox, CreativeNature.nl, 10, Dr. Morley Read, 14, 15, 23e, Gerckens-Photo-Hamburg, 18, 23f, iceeyes198369, 6, Mark Bridger, 4, 23a, back cover, Miles Away Photography, 22, Stephen Mcsweeny, 12, Tom Reichner, 11, Piotr Krzeslak, 7 hedgehog; Superstock: imagebroker.net, 16, 23b.

Every effort has been made to contact copyright holders of material reproduced in this book. Any omissions will be rectified in subsequent printings if notice is given to the publisher.

Contents

What is a barn owl? 4

What does nocturnal mean? 6

Where do barn owls live? 8

What do barn owls eat? 10

How do barn owls find prey? 12

What are owl pellets? 14

What are baby barn owls like? 16

Do barn owls have predators? 18

How can you spot barn owls? 20

Barn owl body map 22

Picture glossary 23

Find out more 24

Index 24

What is a barn owl?

A barn owl is a large bird. Its body is covered in grey or brown feathers.

It has light-coloured feathers on its face.

A barn owl has sharp claws called talons. It has large eyes and a strong **beak**.

You rarely see barn owls during the day because they are **nocturnal**.

What does nocturnal mean?

Animals that are nocturnal are awake at night.

Nocturnal animals sleep during the day.

bat

fox

hedgehog

mouse

Many animals are nocturnal.

Bats, foxes, hedgehogs, and mice are nocturnal.

Where do barn owls live?

Barn owls live in Europe, North America, South America, Africa, Asia, and Australia.

They can live in forests, fields, deserts, farmlands, and even in cities.

Barn owls make nests in trees, caves, and buildings.

They are called barn owls because they often make nests in barns.

What do barn owls eat?

Barn owls hunt for nocturnal animals.

They usually eat small animals, such as mice and bats.

Some barn owls even eat larger animals, such as baby rabbits.

Barn owls also eat other small birds.

How do barn owls find prey?

Barn owls have very good hearing. They listen for **prey**.

Barn owls also have good eyesight. They can see small animals moving in the dark.

Barn owls fly quietly after prey.

They catch prey with their sharp talons.

What are owl pellets?

Owls often swallow their prey whole.

After they eat, they spit out **pellets**.

Pellets are the bones, fur, and feathers of owl prey.

Pellets show the different animals an owl has eaten.

What are baby barn owls like?

Female barn owls lay eggs in springtime.

Owl chicks are covered in **down** shortly after they hatch.

The mother owl brings prey back to the nest to feed the chicks.

Young owls leave the nest after two months.

Do barn owls have predators?

Barn owls have few **predators**.

In some places, raccoons, cats, and larger owls eat barn owl chicks.

Humans can harm barn owls too.

Growing cities and new buildings can make it hard for barn owls to find enough prey to eat.

How can you spot barn owls?

Barn owls are easiest to spot at **dusk**.
Watch for them swooping low over fields.

Owl droppings and pellets can tell you that a nest is nearby.

Listen for barn owl screeches. They can sometimes tell you where a nest is.

Barn owl body map

wing

beak

talon

Picture Glossary

 **beak** a bird's hard jaw

 **down** soft, fluffy feathers of a young bird

 **dusk** time of day when the sun sets

 **nocturnal** awake at night and asleep during the day

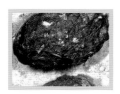 **pellet** bones, fur, and feathers of owl prey

 **predator** animal that hunts other animals for food

 **prey** animal that is hunted by other animals

Find Out More

Books

Owls (Usborne Beginners), Emily Bone (Usborne Publishing Ltd, 2013)

Owl (British Animals), Stephen Savage (Wayland, 2010)

Websites

Discover more about barn owls at:
http://allaboutbirds.org/guide/Barn_Owl/id

Learn more about owls at:
http://bbc.co.uk/nature/life/owl

Index

barns 9
beaks 5, 22
bones 15
buildings 9, 19
cats 18
caves 9
chicks 16, 17, 18
cities 8, 19
claws 5

deserts 8
down 16
droppings 21
dusk 20
eggs 16
eyes 5, 12
farmlands 8
feathers 4, 15
fields 20

food 10, 11
fur 15
grasslands 8
humans 19
nests 9, 17, 21
pellets 14, 15, 21
predators 18
prey 12, 13, 14, 15, 17, 19

rabbits 11
raccoons 18
spring 16
talons 5, 13, 22
trees 9
wings 22
woodlands 8

Please return or renew this item before the latest date shown below

Renewals can be made
by internet   www.fifedirect.org.uk/libraries
in person   at any library in Fife
by phone   08451 55 00 66

Thank you for using your library

male red kangaroo

female red kangaroo

Male red kangaroos are bigger than females.

Red kangaroos live in the desert. They are the biggest **marsupials**. Males can stand more than 2 metres (6.5 feet) tall. That is taller than an adult human. They have short, red-brown fur.

Kangaroo lifestyle

Kangaroos live in small groups, called mobs. As they eat, they listen out for **dingos** and other **predators**. If there is danger, they thump the ground with their feet to warn the others.

This is a mob of kangaroos.

Kangaroos **graze** at
night, when it is cooler.

Red kangaroos eat desert plants.
Their food is tough and wears their
teeth down. When this happens,
more teeth move forward. Then, new
teeth replace them from behind.

Kangaroos move by hopping on their huge back legs and feet. They use their tails for balance as they leap. At top speed, a kangaroo can hop at over 60 kilometres (37 miles) per hour. Hopping uses up less energy than running on all fours.

A kangaroo can cover 8 metres (26 feet) in one leap.

These
kangaroos
are "boxing".

Kangaroos sometimes have to
defend themselves from attack by
other kangaroos. They use their front
paws and look as if they are boxing.
They also try to kick each other.

A new-born kangaroo, or **joey**, is only about the size of a bumblebee. It crawls up its mother's fur and into her **pouch**. Here, it drinks its mother's milk, and grows bigger and stronger.

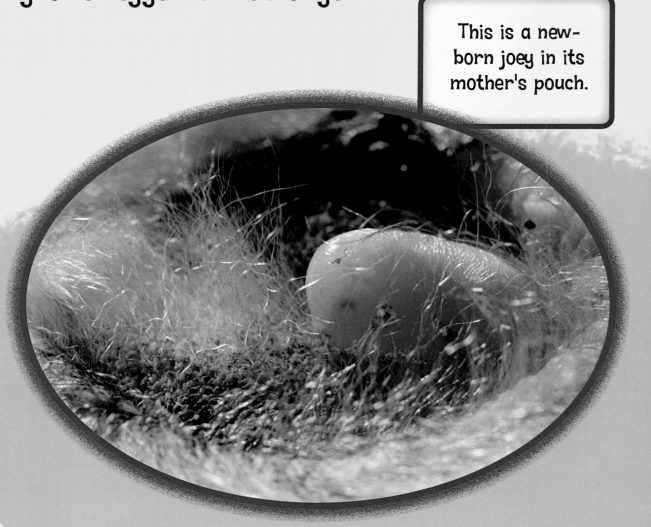

This is a new-born joey in its mother's pouch.

This joey is safely back inside its mother's pouch.

When a joey is about six months old, it comes out of the pouch for the first time. It starts to spend more and more time outside. But it quickly dives back in if it feels frightened.

In captivity

Soon after the Europeans arrived in Australia, they began sending live kangaroos back home. It was a long journey by ship, and many of the kangaroos died. In 1791, a kangaroo was sent to London as a gift for the king.

The first kangaroos caused quite a stir!

These kangaroos live in a wildlife park.

Today, there are thousands of kangaroos in zoos and wildlife parks all around the world. They do very well in **captivity**. Many of these kangaroos have been born in captivity.

Kangaroos today

Kangaroos are an important part of Australian life. They have appeared on stamps and coins, in books and on TV. Many Australian companies have kangaroos as their **logos**. Some sports teams are named after kangaroos.

The Australian coat of arms has a kangaroo on it.

This sign warns drivers to watch out for kangaroos on the roads.

Today, there are millions of kangaroos in Australia. Many are killed on the roads every year. Some cars are fitted with "kangaroo whistles". The sounds help to stop kangaroos from crossing the road.

Scientists are still finding out more about kangaroos. At Riversleigh in Australia, they discovered the fossils of **extinct** kangaroos. One had curved, fang-like teeth. The scientists nicknamed it the "fangaroo".

The fossils at Riversleigh are millions of years old.

This is a model of a giant kangaroo that became extinct around 30,000 years ago.

A fossil of a giant kangaroo has been found. It was three times the size of a modern kangaroo. In 2014, scientists discovered that it was too big to hop. It walked on its back legs instead.

Kangaroo timeline

1770

Captain Cook and his crew sail to Australia and see kangaroos.

1771

Banks brings a kangaroo skin to London. It is stuffed and put on display.

1789

British officer, Watkin Tench, writes a detailed description of a kangaroo.

1791

A live kangaroo arrives in London as a gift for the king.

1828

A British scientist, John Morgan, tames a kangaroo. It follows him around like a dog.

1908

The kangaroo features on the Australian coat of arms.

1966

Scientists decide that the kangaroos Banks saw were eastern grey kangaroos.

2000

At the Sydney Olympic Games, the Australian team's logo is a boxing kangaroo.

2014

Scientists discover that the extinct giant short-faced kangaroo probably could not hop but walked instead.

Glossary

boomerang curved stick that spins and turns in flight; some boomerangs are made to return to the thrower

captivity condition of being kept in a cage, often in zoos or wildlife parks

coral reef type of land made up of the hardened bodies of corals; corals are small, colourful sea creatures

dingo wild dog that lives in Australia

extinct no longer living; an extinct animal is one that has died out, with no more of its kind

graze feed on grass and plants

indigenous native to a place

joey young kangaroo

logo symbol of an organization's brand

marsupial group of mammals in which the females feed and carry their young in pouches

pouch flap of skin that looks like a pocket in which some animals carry their young

predator animal that hunts other animals for food

rodent mammal with long front teeth used for gnawing; rats, mice and squirrels are rodents

Find out more

Books

Big Red Kangaroo, Claire Saxby (Walker Books Australia, 2015)

Fantastic Facts about Kangaroos, Miles Merchant (CreateSpace, 2015)

The Life Cycle of a Kangaroo, Amy Austen (PowerKids Press, 2015)

Websites

animals.nationalgeographic.com/animals/mammals/red-kangaroo

Facts and figures about kangaroos from the National Geographic website.

animals.sandiegozoo.org/animals/kangaroo-wallaby

Meet the kangaroos at San Diego Zoo.

www.bbc.co.uk/nature/life/Macropod

Information, photos and videos about kangaroos and wallabies.

Index

Australia 4, 5, 22, 24, 25
  Riversleigh 26

Banks, Joseph 5, 6, 7, 14
boxing 19

Cook, Captain James 5, 7

food 17

hopping 4, 6, 18, 27

indigenous Australians 6, 10, 12, 13

joey (baby kangaroo) 20, 21

kangaroos
  eastern grey 14, 25
  fossil 26, 27
  in captivity 22, 23
  red 15, 17, 25
  whistles 25

marsupials 9, 15
mobs 16

pouch 9, 20, 21
predators 16

size 15
skin 7, 8, 11
speed 18
stories 12, 13

teeth 11, 17

wild kangaroos 14, 15, 25

Raintree is an imprint of Capstone Global Library Limited, a company incorporated in England and Wales having its registered office at 264 Banbury Road, Oxford OX2 7DY – Registered company number: 6695582

www.raintree.co.uk
myorders@raintree.co.uk

Edited by Linda Staniford
Designed by Philippa Jenkins
Original illustrations © Capstone Global Library Limited 2016
Picture research by Morgan Walters
Production by Victoria Fitzgerald
Originated by Capstone Global Library Ltd

ISBN 978 1 474 71451 8 (hardback)
20 19 18 17 16
10 9 8 7 6 5 4 3 2 1

ISBN 978 1 474 71460 0 (paperback)
21 20 19 18 17
10 9 8 7 6 5 4 3 2 1

British Library Cataloguing in Publication Data
A full catalogue record for this book is available from the British Library.

Acknowledgements
We would like to thank the following for permission to reproduce photographs: Alamy: David Reed, 24; Bridgeman Images: National Library of Australia, Canberra, Australia, 7, Natural History Museum, London, UK, 6; Corbis: Charles & Josette Lenars, 12, Hulton-Deutsch Collection, 22; Dreamstime: Jan Pokorný, Cover, Sandbread, 18; Getty Images: Auscape/UIG, 13, Hulton Archive, 5, Mitsuaki/Iwago, 20, Photolibrary, 4, Yva Momatiuk & John Eastcott, 15; Glow Images: Deposit Photos, 23, Steve Bowman, 10; iStockphoto: Houshmand Rabbani, 14; Newscom: STR/REUTERS, 27, TUNS/picture alliance/Arco Images G, 19; Science Source: Wayne G. Lawler, 26; Shutterstock: Dioscoro L. Dioticio, 16, Gianna Stadelmyer, 17, nattanan726, 9, shelley kirby, 21, Totajla, 25; The Trustees of the British Museum, 11; Wikimedia: ArtDaily.com, 8.

We would like to thank Michael Bright for his invaluable help in the preparation of this book.

Every effort has been made to contact copyright holders of material reproduced in this book. Any omissions will be rectified in subsequent printings if notice is given to the publisher.

Printed and bound in the United Kingdom.

FABULOUS ANIMALS

ry of the

roo

eri

a Capstone company — publishers for children

This sign tells boat drivers to slow down for manatees.

MANATEE ZONE

IDLE SPEED
NO WAKE

PERMIT NO.92-037 ALL YEAR 62N 22.011 FAC

Some parts of Florida are watery **reserves** where boats are not allowed. Manatees can live safely there. In other areas, boats have to drive very slowly.

Who is helping Florida manatees?

People in some wildlife parks help injured or sick Florida manatees. They care for them until they are well, then they set the manatees free.

People are putting this manatee back into the sea now that it is better.

Save the Manatee is a **charity** that tells people about manatees and why they need help. It protects manatees and the places where they live.

Charities work with *scientists* to find out more about Florida manatees.

How can you help?

It is important to know that Florida manatees are in danger. Then you can learn how to help save them. Read, watch, and find out all you can about Florida manatees.

This class is doing a project on manatees.

Here are some things you can do
to help.

- Join a **charity** such as Save the
  Manatee. Can you raise money to
  save manatees?
- Visit wildlife parks or **reserves** where
  Florida manatees live safely. In some
  places you can even pay to swim
  with the manatees.

The future for Florida manatees

We must stop **pollution** in the sea and rivers and make sure we drive fast boats with care. If we do not, manatees may become **extinct**.

If there are too many people in Florida, will there be room for manatees?

Many people are working hard to save manatees. They hope that the number of Florida manatees will begin to grow if they are protected.

Let's hope that people will still be able to see these animals in the future.

Florida manatee facts

- Manatees are related to elephants. Their bones are like an elephant's, they have little hair, and their top lip moves a bit like a mini-trunk.
- Manatees can live for more than 60 years.
- A big manatee eats a lot of plants. It eats the same amount as 200 lettuces every day.
- Manatees can hold their breath underwater for several minutes before they need to come up for air.

More books to read

Gentle Manatees, Kathleen Martin-James (Lerner, 2005)

I'm a Manatee, John Lithgow (Simon & Schuster Children's Publishing, 2004)

Websites

To find out more about Save the Manatee, visit their website:

www.savethemanatee.org

Glossary

calf baby manatee

charity group that collects money and gives help to animals or people in need

coast area of land where it meets the sea. Beaches are found along a coast.

extinct when all the animals in a species die out and the species no longer exists

female animal that can become a mother when it grows up. Women and girls are female people.

flippers front arms of a manatee

herbivore animal that only eats plants

mammal animal that feeds its babies on the mother's milk and has some hair on its body

migrate move to a different place to live for part of the year

pollution when something makes the land, rivers, oceans, or air dirty

reserve area where animals are protected

scientist person who studies the world around them

species group of animals that look similar and can have babies together

Index

babies 12–13
boats 16, 23, 28
breathing 12, 16, 30

calves 12–13, 21, 31
charities 25, 27, 31
coasts 8, 31

dangers 14–19, 21, 26

extinction 4–5, 28, 31

females 12–13, 21, 31
fishing lines and nets
  17, 22
flippers 7, 10–11, 31
Florida 8–9
food 10–11, 13,
  18–19, 30

herbivores 10, 31

laws 22

mammals 12, 31
migration 9, 31
mouth 6

numbers 20–21, 29

plants 10–11, 13,
  18–19, 30
pollution 19, 22, 28, 31

reserves 23, 27, 31

Save the Manatee 25, 27,
  30
skin 6, 16
species 4, 31
swimming 7

tail 7
teeth 11

wildlife parks 24, 27

www.heinemann.co.uk/library
Visit our website to find out more information about Heinemann Library books.

To order:
☎ Phone 44 (0) 1865 888066
🖹 Send a fax to 44 (0) 1865 314091
💻 Visit the Heinemann Bookshop at www.heinemann.co.uk/library to browse our
catalogue and order online.

First published in Great Britain by Heinemann Library,
Halley Court, Jordan Hill, Oxford OX2 8EJ, part of
Harcourt Education.
Heinemann is a registered trademark of Harcourt
Education Ltd.

Editorial: Kate Bellamy, Diyan Leake, Cassie Mayer,
  and Katie Shepherd
Design: Michelle Lisseter and Ron Kamen
Illustrations: Bridge Creative Services
Cartographer: Vickie Taylor at International Mapping
Picture research: Hannah Taylor and Fiona Orbell
Production: Duncan Gilbert

Origination: Chroma Graphics (Overseas) Pte. Ltd
Printed and bound in China by South
China Printing Co. Ltd

The paper used to print this book comes from
sustainable resources.

10 digit ISBN 0 431 11425 0 (hardback)
13 digit ISBN 978 0 431 11425 5
10 09 08 07 06
10 9 8 7 6 5 4 3 2 1

10 digit ISBN 0 431 11433 1 (paperback)
13 digit ISBN 978 0 431 11433 0
11 10 09 08 07
10 9 8 7 6 5 4 3 2 1

British Library Cataloguing in Publication Data
Spilsbury, Louise and Richard
Save the Florida manatee. – (Save our animals!)
599.5' 5' 09759
A full catalogue record for this book is available from
the British Library.

Acknowledgements
The publishers would like to thank the following for
permission to reproduce photographs: Ardea pp. **4** top
(Y A Betrand), **5** top left (J Rajput); Corbis pp. **6**
(B D Cole), **27** (MacDuff Everton); Digital Vision p. **5**
middle; Empics/AP Photo pp. **17** (P Cosgrove), **24**
(SeaWorld Orlando); Florida Fish & Wildlife
Conservation Commission p. **22**; FLPA/Minden Pictures
pp. **11**, **15** (F Bavendam); Naturepl.com pp. **4** bottom
left (M Carwardine), **9**, **12** (D Perrine), **14** (P Scoones),
16, **18** (J Foot); Nick Nottestad p. **26**; Oxford Scientific
pp. **4** middle, **5** top right, **7**, **13** (G Soury), **23**, **25**;
Photolibrary.com pp. **21**, **28**; Still Pictures pp. **5** bottom,
10 (Dr. H Barnett), **19** (A & F Michler), **29** (D Faulkner).

Cover photograph of Florida manatee reproduced with
permission of Corbis/Kennan Ward.

The publishers would like to thank staff at Save the
Manatee for their assistance in the preparation of
this book.

Every effort has been made to contact copyright
holders of any material reproduced in this book.
Any omissions will be rectified in subsequent
printings if notice is given to the publishers.

SAVE OUR ANIMALS!

Manatee

Spilsbury

Heinemann
LIBRARY

I don't like my baby sister very much.

I get cross and shout at her. Now Mum is cross with me. I don't like my baby sister very much.

Dad and I are looking after Megan.

Dad and I are looking after Megan today. She is eight weeks old now and smiles at me.

I show him what to do.

Dad is not very good
at changing nappies.
I show him what to do.

My baby sister is growing up.

Megan is nine months old now. She likes to play with me and I read her stories.

I love my
baby sister.

I love my baby sister. When she
is bigger we will have lots of fun.

Index

baby 6, 8, 10, 11, 12

clothes 8

Dad 8, 12, 16, 17

Grandma 10, 11

hospital 10, 12

Megan 13, 16, 18

Mum 6, 7, 10, 12, 13, 15

nappies 17

picture 11, 13

sister 12, 13, 14, 15, 18, 19

tummy 6

Notes to Parents

It is hard to exaggerate the level of stress that a child will experience when they realise that another member of the family is about to be born. During the mother's pregnancy, the child will feel resentful at all the new things that are bought and the excitement that everyone feels for a person who does not yet exist. Once the baby is born, the limelight passes from the child to the new arrival, and the child, (particularly if an only child), may feel completely unloved and ignored. Many children revert to babyish speech and behaviour as a way of seeking attention.

Preparing children well in advance is absolutely vital. From the age of two or three, the possibility of the child having brothers and sisters can be talked about. The child should not actually be told about the expected baby until a few months before the birth. Nine months is a very long time for a small child to wait. At this stage all the positive aspects of a sibling can be emphasised. The child can help the parents prepare a room for the baby and their opinion can be sought on what colour clothes or choice of equipment should be bought. All children should enjoy the thought of having someone new to play with.

Mum's departure to hospital should be discussed well beforehand. The child should know who will look after them when this happens and that Dad will come and tell them the news first of all. When Mum returns home with the new baby the child should be encouraged to look upon themself as an important helper and made to feel that their contribution to helping Mum and Dad with the baby is very important.

• When buying things for the new baby, the child should also be included with little presents.

• Friends, grandparents and other members of the family should be encouraged to give the child as much attention as the new baby.

My name is Bethan.
This book tells you about
my new baby sister.

Full Moon

When the Moon grows bigger from night to night, we say it is waxing. When the Moon grows smaller, we say it is waning.

Looking at the Moon

People on Earth have looked at the night sky for thousands of years. A scientist invented the telescope about 400 years ago. It made things look bigger and nearer. This helped people see the night sky more clearly.

The Hubble Space Telescope takes pictures in space.

People who study space and the stars are called astronomers. They look at the sky through big telescopes. Some telescopes are on mountains. They see the sky clearly.

In 1990 scientists sent the huge Hubble Space Telescope into space. It takes photos and sends them back to Earth.

Exploring the Moon

Scientists send probes into space to look at the Moon close up. The probes take photos of the Moon. Some probes have landed on the surface.

WOW!

Today a spacecraft flies around the Moon taking photos. It is called the *Lunar Reconnaissance Orbiter*. The photos will help scientists make a map of the Moon.

In 1998 a tiny space probe went to look for ice in craters on the Moon. It was only 140 cm wide! The probe crashed at the end of its journey.

Lunar Prospector

People on the Moon

The Moon is the only part of the solar system that people have visited. The first person to land on the Moon was Neil Armstrong in 1969. He travelled there on a spacecraft called *Apollo 11*. Another explorer in *Apollo 11* called Buzz Aldrin walked on the Moon, too.

The men left their footprints on the Moon. The footprints will stay there for millions of years. This is because there is no wind or rain on the Moon.

A space explorer is called an astronaut.
Twelve astronauts have visited the Moon.
They brought Moon rocks back to Earth.

Eclipses

The Moon travels around the Earth.
The Earth orbits the Sun. Sometimes
the Moon, the Earth and the Sun all
line up in a row.

The Moon can
turn red or
orange during
an eclipse.

When the Earth is between the Sun and the Moon, it makes a shadow on the Moon. This is called a lunar eclipse. The photo shows how the Moon disappears when the shadow of the Earth falls on it.

Make moon phases

What you need

4 chocolate cream-filled
   biscuits (or round crackers
   and cream cheese)

Lolly stick or plastic knife
Sheet of paper

What to do

1. Twist the top of each biscuit.
Try not to pull off the cream.

2. Use the lolly stick or plastic
knife to scrape off the cream
filling. Make your biscuits
match the pictures here.
They show the shapes of four
of the phases of the Moon.

3. Arrange the biscuits on
the sheet of paper in order.
Write the name of the phase
under each biscuit.

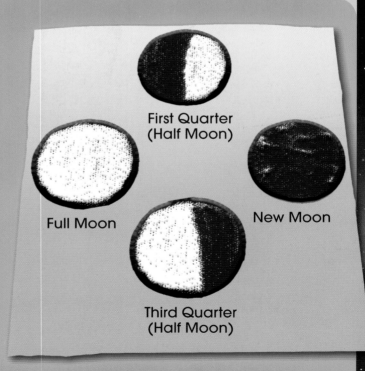

First Quarter
(Half Moon)

Full Moon

New Moon

Third Quarter
(Half Moon)

Useful words

asteroid
A big rock that orbits the Sun.
An asteroid can be just a
few metres across, or
hundreds of kilometres wide.

comet
A ball of rock, dust and ice
that orbits the Sun.

core
The centre of a star, planet
or moon.

crater
A hole in the surface of the
Moon made by a large
rocky object hitting it. →

eclipse
There is an eclipse when
one object in space passes
in front of another and hides
it. In a lunar eclipse, the
Earth blocks the Sun's light.

lunar
To do with the Moon.

orbit
To move around
another object.

planet
A large object in space that
orbits the Sun or another star.

Find out more

Websites

www.planetsforkids.org/moon.
html

www.esa.int/esaKIDSen/
Planetsandmoons.html

www.spacekids.co.uk/themoon

Books

Fact Cat Moon, Alice Harman
(Wayland, 2015)

First Encyclopedia of Space,
Paul Dowswell (Usborne, 2010)

First Fabulous Facts Space,
Anita Ganeri (Ladybird, 2014)

Index

asteroids 6, 23
astronauts 18–19
astronomers 15

craters 10, 11, 17, 23

dwarf planets 7

eclipses 20–21, 23

light 4, 5, 6, 12

maps 16
mountains 11

orbits 4, 5, 6, 7, 11, 12, 20, 23

phases of the Moon 12–13
planets 4, 6, 7, 8, 23
probes 16–17

shadows 12, 21
spacecraft 16–17, 18
stars 6, 15
Sun 4, 5, 6, 7, 11, 12, 20, 21

telescopes 14–15

waxing and waning 13

Published in paperback in 2017 by Wayland

© 2017 Brown Bear Books Ltd

Wayland
An imprint of Hachette Children's Group
Part of Hodder & Stoughton
Carmelite House
50 Victoria Embankment
London EC4Y 0DZ
An Hachette UK Company
www.hachette.co.uk
www.hachettechildrens.co.uk

ISBN 978 1 5263 0292 2

Brown Bear Books Ltd
First Floor, 9–17 St. Albans Place
London N1 0NX

Author: Mary-Jane Wilkins
Consultant: Giles Sparrow, Fellow of the Royal
Astronomical Society
Picture Researcher: Clare Newman
Illustrations: Supriya Sahai
Designer: Melissa Roskell
Design Manager: Keith Davis
Editorial Director: Lindsey Lowe
Children's Publisher: Anne O'Daly

Printed in Malaysia

Our Solar System

THE MOON

Mary-Jane Wilkins
Consultant: Giles Sparrow, FRAS

WAYLAND
www.waylandbooks.co.uk